Being 21

Towards greater self-understanding in 21 questions

Lynn B. Mann

BB

Being Books

First Edition

ISBN: 978-1-8381628-1-8

Published by Being Books

Printed by KDP Print

Cover and interior design:
Raspberry Creative Type, Edinburgh

For

Evie,

Wishing you all that you wish for yourself,

Happy 21st

Love Joanne x

Connect with me:

Email sign-up: stuff@lynnbmann.com

Facebook: Lynn B. Mann and/or Being 21

Instagram: lynnb.mann and/or being.21

Twitter: @LynnBMann1

Website: lynnbmann.com

About the Author

I've been writing for years, alongside twenty-two different jobs, before becoming a counsellor/therapist, then running two businesses. My main focus recently has been writing a larger self-development book, to be published in 2021. *Being 21* grew out of that. Also, as my son and his girlfriend were approaching twenty-one, it got me thinking about this stage in life as the start of our self-development journey. I wanted to create something meaningful for this time of transition.

I love my life, but I've struggled, made mistakes, learned lessons the hard way, questioned myself, challenged myself, and generally wrestled with life: trying to manage it and mould it into what I felt it could be. In my writing, I offer up only my take on things, hoping it might help others in their own struggles to make sense of it all. I believe it's our most fundamental purpose as human beings. It's what we're all meant to do.

Introduction

In this book there are twenty-one questions for you to ask yourself. They go from looking at the broader, more general aspects of your life, to delving deeper into yourself as you work through them. The aim of this isn't for you to immediately know all the answers – it's to introduce you to a process of questioning which will help you begin to develop greater self-understanding.

There are no right or wrong answers, just what's true for you. You might find it helpful to come back to the questions over a few weeks or months, or at various times throughout your twenties, to see how your thoughts and feelings change. You'll start to notice that you have more self-awareness over time.

Each question has some additional sub-questions: these are just prompts to help you in thinking about the main question, and there is plenty of space around them for you to take notes as thoughts come to you. Or you might also want to use a notebook to write out your answers more fully. Often, we don't really know what our thoughts and feelings are, until we're asked a question, or until we try writing them down.

Take time to reflect on each question. Some will resonate with you more than others, while some might make you feel uncomfortable, confused, or frustrated, if you don't immediately know what you think or feel about it. That's all part of the process. You will be pushing out of the comfort zones that you developed as a teenager, which is a necessary part of growing and changing as a person.

Why would you want to do something that makes you uncomfortable? Because the alternative is to wait until life pushes you out of your comfort zones at a time when you're not choosing it and not in control of it. Instead, you can decide to begin the process yourself and, through it, become more capable of dealing with whatever life throws at you by understanding yourself better. As well as creating confidence and resilience, this can also improve your relationships and strengthen your work skills. Doing this now is an investment in your future.

On the pages following each question, you'll find some of my thoughts. They are just my take on things from my life experiences, developed over time. I hope these might help you on your journey towards greater self-understanding. Also, at the end of the book, you'll find examples of answers from others aged between twenty and twenty-two. These are from an online survey I conducted while researching this book and also from conversations with others in this age group. As you'll see, there's a wide variety of responses. Considering whether you agree or disagree with them might guide you in finding your own thoughts and feelings about the subject or might just be of interest.

It's a long time since I was where you are in life now. Even so, I vividly remember a lot of how I felt and what was going on in my head. The years of our early twenties are such an intense time in our lives; they become etched in our memory. It's the time we begin to map out what our adult life might look like. We're likely to have to make big decisions around career or studying or where we'll live, and about relationships.

I felt like a bit of a mess in my early twenties, although I acted like I had it all together. I was struggling with an eating disorder, was lost career-wise, and had a lot of fear and anxiety around life's uncertainties. I also had great friends, and lots of fun times and adventures. I remember being full of questions, but I wasn't finding many answers, and I often felt like a child pretending to be a grown-up. By twenty-one, I'd already had several different jobs and had started then left college. Sometimes, I lived in a rented flat, and sometimes, back at home, and I was mixing in new social circles as well as having my old friends. Everything felt new and different, exciting and terrifying.

My motivation for writing this book comes partly from the fact that I wish I'd known then what I know now. Not in terms of how things would work out in my life – I just wish, instead of looking outside myself, that I'd realised the answers were actually within me. I didn't know that I needed to get into the habit of asking myself questions to understand myself better and to be more able to point myself in whatever the right direction is *for me*. That's what I hope this book does for you. I hope these questions will help you live your life in a way that keeps you healthy – mentally, emotionally, and physically – and that gives you satisfaction, fulfilment, and joy.

Life is difficult. You will have ups and downs, happy times and heartbreaks, accomplishments and frustrations. Sometimes, you might feel lost and alone, and sometimes, you might feel safe and secure. Nothing is guaranteed, and often, things are unpredictable. You'll never have all the answers, but by being willing to learn a process of self-questioning and answering yourself honestly, you'll feel more able to cope with many of the uncertainties of life. You'll feel more capable and secure in knowing that you can look to your true self for answers. You'll be fully experiencing what this crazy, wonderful human life is about. Being yourself is absolutely the best way to experience it. You don't need to 'fix' yourself or 'find' yourself; you just need to understand yourself better and, crucially, accept what you find.

I hope your twenties are a brilliant decade for you. That you soak it all up and learn from it all. I hope that you come to know your true self and live your life authentically, as *you*. The reality is that some people will love that you, some won't, and most will be indifferent – which would be the case *whoever* you were in the world, so you may as well just be unapologetically yourself.

If you only do that in life, and nothing else, your life will already be more successful than a lot of people's. Many don't push through the fear or discomfort of trying to know themselves better, so they end up living life as who they think they're meant to be, rather than who they actually are. You are already stronger, braver, and more capable than you think you are. And you can prove that to yourself as you work through these twenty-one questions.

You only get one life, and believe me, it goes by in a flash. The sooner you start to live your life as your true self, the sooner you'll begin to create a full, big, life and, ultimately, come to experience the feeling that you're fulfilling your unique potential as a human being.

Does it depend on circumstances,
or who you're with?

✶

Does it depend on others' behaviour
towards you?

✶

Do you feel like you're still establishing
yourself as an adult?

✶

What advice would you give to
your sixteen-year-old self about the
next five years to twenty-one?

Question 1

Do you feel like you are an adult?

Obviously, becoming an adult isn't something that happens overnight. It's a process. One that speeds up as you approach your twenties, especially if going to university or college, or starting your first full-time job, or leaving home are part of your life experiences around this time. The more you take on responsibilities independently of others, the more you feel thrust into adulthood. And the more you're likely to have to make choices and decisions for yourself.

There's no manual for adulthood: if you asked five different adults for tips in navigating the transition, you'd get five different sets of answers. Every single person has a unique combination of life experiences, at every stage in their lives. That life path to date, combined with your own personality and character traits, means that someone else's road map might take you way off the path that's right for you. However, this doesn't mean you can't learn from others' experiences and the things they've discovered. Take them all in but, at the same time, start to figure out what might be useful for you personally, and what wouldn't be so useful.

This stage of life can feel exciting and liberating but also sometimes terrifying and confusing. Whatever you feel now is all part of the process of creating your individual identity and laying down the foundations of who you'll be in adulthood. Taking some time to reflect on the questions throughout this book and coming up with your own questions about who your truest self is and what you might want your life to look like can support you in this time of transition. The process can help you to create a vision for your way forward.

As you go through this book, and this stage of life, be kind to yourself. Most of us have underlying feelings of somehow not being 'enough' or of being flawed in one way or another. As you think about your answers to the rest of these questions, I hope you'll begin to accept yourself more, whatever you come to learn about yourself.

What issues seem most detrimental to the peace and happiness of your generation?

✶

Are they around mental, emotional, or physical health and wellbeing?

✶

Are they what's going on in your immediate environment, or in the wider world?

Question 2

What would you say are the major concerns of your generation?

Every generation has its burden to bear, its common issues to deal with. For people around your age though, it feels like there's a hell of a lot going on just now that you might be concerned about. But there's also a growing number of you acting on those concerns. It gives me huge hope for the future when I see the compassionate action and passionate vocalising that is born of your generation's need to respond.

Your concerns might be around such huge issues as the environment, mental health, poverty, equality, or another major challenge that our society is facing.

It can feel overwhelming. However, even something as simple as just learning more about an issue can be empowering. There's a sense of relief in realising there's more you can do to influence things than you might have thought.

Even if it doesn't feel like it right now, you as an individual can make so much of a difference. Whatever one person does has a ripple effect out into the world that can influence change in ways we sometimes don't see. Anything you can do to begin to address your own concerns will matter. Even if it's something small, it starts taking you in a new direction, one step at a time, which then leads to the next thing, then the next thing ...

In doing this, you get into the habit of channelling your energy into positive action instead of going round in circles with your thoughts and feelings, which could just leave you feeling helpless.

If you talk with others, you might also come up with things you can do collectively to create the change that you want to happen. It's amazing what can be achieved by collaboration.

What would be most beneficial on
a large scale, or more individually?

✶

Would it be a solution to some
of the concerns you identified in
Question 2?

✶

Are any of these things that you
can make happen or help
to make happen?

Question 3

What would be the best thing that could happen to your generation just now?

When I've asked people this question, I've been surprised that the answers often shift away from the global concerns that come up in response to Question 2 and move towards more personal issues: the dominance of social media and the materialism, consumerism, and superficiality that many of you see around you. I see that too, and I think your generation will be the ones to change it, because you seem more aware of it and sense that you can do something about it.

My thoughts on Question 2 apply here too: you might be surprised by how much you, as an individual, can do to help create the changes you'd like to see. Whatever they are, there are likely to be people already working towards them. Seek them out and see what you can do to be a part of it. Most change is brought about by a network of individual concerns that a great many people share, leading to individual actions, which together create a net of influence in the world.

When it comes to things that affect you more personally, try to figure out your own thoughts, feelings, frustrations, and desires about it. What exactly would you like to happen? A useful exercise is to break down what you want to happen into the stages or steps that are necessary to achieve it and write them down. This can make it more manageable and seem more achievable. Often, something that seems like too big a thing to tackle is really just a series of small things. That's how we all create the world around us.

Are they specific or general?

✷

Can you do something to prevent them or lessen the chances of them happening?

✷

Are there any certainties that you wish you had in areas like career, health, relationships, or family?

Question 4

What are your biggest fears for yourself about how the rest of your life might work out?

At your age, I remember having big fears around what I would end up doing career-wise, whether I would meet someone I'd want to spend my life with, and if I would ever sort myself out! When I look back on that time now, I wish I'd realised that it's just a stage of life – one we all go through. It's part of becoming an adult – realising that your life is now more or less in your own hands, and you're now responsible for the majority of decisions about how you live it. You might get advice and guidance from lots of angles, but ultimately, the choices you make are up to you. It's one of the best and worst things about this time in your life – when you realise that your future is in your hands.

When you're looking at the different areas of your life and no outcomes seem certain, it can make you feel paralysed in making decisions. Lack of certainty can be very unsettling. Believe me, though, it doesn't change much as you go through life! The certainties you wish for just shift focus – to your health, or your children's lives, or finances ...

I've discovered that the best way to deal with it is by getting comfortable with the fact that there is always a certain amount of uncertainty and fear in life, focussing instead on what can be done to tackle or minimise the fears.

With the ones you can't do anything about, try to spend less of your time and attention engaging with them. Even if they're still in the background, you can choose to direct your attention towards the things that you can do something about instead – and also towards all that's good in your life, towards your goals and plans, or the things that bring you happiness.

And by doing this repeatedly, you can actually rewire your brain! Neural pathways are laid down and become more ingrained each time you repeat a behaviour, such as shifting your focus towards positive thoughts. Over time, it'll become more automatic, because it's what your brain expects to happen; it's got the pathway there to follow. This is called neuroplasticity.

The downside is that this works as much for developing negative habits as it does for positive ones. That's why it's difficult to break bad habits and stick to new ones. It's completely possible though. You can consciously direct your energy and attention into behaviours that help you grow and develop then keep repeating them consciously until they become more automatic.

Big or small things?

✶

Are these things that you worry about
on a regular basis?

✶

Is there a common theme,
like career or relationships?

Question 5

What are you most scared of in life just now?

Many of our fears as we become an adult are around our capabilities – not dealing with things well or not making the most of our life. When it comes to our more immediate fears, there is often a lot more we can do about them than we think. Sometimes, taking any action, however small, towards dealing with that fear is enough to get the momentum going for you – to get you to a place where you feel able to tackle whatever is behind the fear. As you do this, or until you do, maybe you can reframe the things you're scared of to get a different perspective on them.

For instance, if there's a big emotional charge to what you're scared of, try doing whatever it takes to dial down your emotional response. That could be anything: a walk, a run, sleep, food, consciously thinking about something else for a bit, or doing a mundane task that you have to concentrate on. Then, when you're in a more relaxed state, reflect on your fears from a calmer place. It may also help to talk to people you trust about your fears, when you're in that calmer place, and maybe brainstorm some potential solutions. Look for things you can do now, or in the short term, that might help to diminish your fears as you create a longer-term plan to deal with them. Often just talking to someone about things can be a relief.

Noticing the negative thought patterns attached to your fears can also help diminish them. Notice how much your thinking fuels your fears. Sometimes, you come to realise that your fears are ungrounded or that you're doing more to alleviate them than you'd initially thought. Having fears doesn't need to stop you pushing forwards in creating the life that you want for yourself.

I often remind myself of the title of a book I bought many years ago: *Feel the Fear and Do It Anyway*, by Susan Jeffers. Obviously, this phrase isn't a mandate to do things that might risk your health and wellbeing – it's more a statement of the fact that being scared of something doesn't automatically mean we shouldn't do it. If things we feel scared of doing can lead to big rewards, great life experiences, or fulfilling our dreams, we can push on and do what we want to do, in spite of our fear – proving to ourselves that we can do things that feel difficult for us.

Often, we'll look back later and think, 'What was I worried about?' Tackling some of your fears can leave you feeling really proud of yourself. It can be a liberating experience.

Do you look for those lessons,
either at the time or afterwards?

✷

With challenges, do you tend to
tackle them as soon as possible,
or put them off for as long as possible?

Question 6

Do you think that difficulties in life can teach you valuable lessons?

Challenges in life, however tough, are what help us to grow as a person and develop our capabilities for dealing with future difficulties. The more capable we feel, the more likely we are to explore, push our boundaries, stretch our comfort zones, and deal directly with life's inevitable hurdles and hassles. In a nutshell, the more capable we feel, the bigger the range of life experiences we'll have which, in turn, helps us to grow even more as a person. It's a process. Stretching your current capabilities develops your future capabilities and builds adaptability, courage, and self-esteem.

I only learned a few years ago that this is called a 'growth mindset'. With a growth mindset we believe that we are able to change and grow. Challenges become opportunities to learn. The opposite is having a 'fixed mindset' where you feel that people's traits and abilities are not changeable. With a fixed mindset you're more likely to think that you're just naturally good, or bad, at certain things. It's a static perspective: you see things as black or white. With a growth mindset you realise that all of us can develop our skills and capabilities throughout life. This is part of the neuroplasticity I talked about after Question 4 – the way we can rewire our brains throughout our lives, even into old age.

The really good news is that you can change from a fixed mindset to a growth mindset just by seeing life's challenges as an opportunity to grow. Doing what people with a growth mindset do is what develops the growth mindset in you. How good is that! You don't need to avoid life's difficulties – you can take a deep breath and walk towards them, knowing that you're likely to come out of the other side a stronger, wiser person from all that you have overcome.

Author, Susan Jeffers, says, 'Security in life isn't having things, it's handling things.' I remind myself of this often, and I expand what I feel I'm capable of, over and over, each time that I tackle life's inevitable challenges rather than turning away from them.

Is it just being able to do
what you want, when you want?

✶

Does it just mean physical freedom?

✶

What about mental, emotional,
or spiritual freedoms?

Question 7

What do you think having freedom is?

Freedom is a big and emotive concept. We all want it or think we want it, but some types of freedom bring unwanted baggage: feelings of insecurity, uncertainty, or anxiety. There are different kinds of freedom, and there's always a trade-off between freedoms, commitments, and responsibilities.

Think about wanting to be free of any responsibility in life. Is that possible, or even desirable? What would the cost of that freedom be? Sometimes, it's a case of 'be careful what you wish for'.

Freedom is a powerful goal, especially when it comes to feeling free mentally, emotionally, and spiritually – even while still having the responsibilities, commitments, or structures that we need to live within for whatever reason.

Feelings of freedom come and go in different situations and at different stages in our lives. The most consistent, fundamental sense of freedom we can have is to feel that we know ourselves and can be ourselves – unapologetically. At the same time, we must bear in mind the freedom of others to also be themselves, live in their truth, and do what they feel they need to do in following their own path. Throughout our lives, we have a balancing act to master, pursuing our own freedoms at the same time as respecting and allowing for the freedoms of the other people in our life.

Our freedom to be our true self comes in asking ourselves the hard questions about who we really are, what we want to experience in our life, and what we want to create in the world then giving ourselves the time and space to explore the answers, or let them become apparent, and being honest with ourselves about what is true for us. Then we put one foot in front of the other on the path that is ours alone.

Is it about one aspect of your life
or a whole series of things?

Is it reaching a certain place in
who you are, or how you live?

Is it in how you'll look,
how you'll feel, or about
other symbols of success?

Question 8

What does a successful life look like to you?

Often, the answer people give to this question is 'being happy' – but few break that down into exactly what would make them happy. The trick to finding happiness is figuring out what makes you happy. Not just momentarily – ice cream, some alcohol, or a hug can achieve that – but in a more consistent way. And also by widening your definition of happiness.

Happiness isn't just feelings of being happy. In a broader definition, it includes feeling content, safe, or needed and wanted, doing work you love, being secure in your relationships, or feeling that you can be yourself and express who you really are. When happiness is more than just a feeling that comes and goes, you can build on what is satisfying in your life to create a deeper undercurrent of happiness. You then feel you're living a life that feels successful – by your definition of success. Others will have their own definitions and might not relate to yours, but if you become a seeker of what will create longer term happiness, you'll come to understand what a successful life looks like for you.

For me, feeling successful in life has nearly always been about love and freedom. The type of freedom I just spoke about after Question 7 – being myself. It took me a while to figure this out though. I got there by trying to get to know what I wanted my life to be about, and how I wanted to live it, and then by getting better at just being myself. I'm getting more successful at that every day. Also, loving, caring relationships that are a two-way street and feed my soul feel like a huge part of a successful life to me. I feel so fortunate to have some of those relationships in my life. I value them, so I give them my time and attention.

Author, Glennon Doyle, believes that 'the point of being human is not to be happy, it's to feel everything'. For most people, that's a scary thought. Often, we think that if we really feel our feelings, we won't be able to handle them. I've spent years trying to get better at doing this. Sometimes, it feels easier than others. I think the key to it is what I'll go on to talk about in my thoughts on Question 15. It's in awareness and acceptance of your feelings and of yourself for having them. Then you can more fully experience them without fearing that they will overwhelm you, and you get to live your own definition of a happy life.

Can you imagine how you might
have changed by then?

✶

How do you think your attitude to life
and success might change after a
few decades of living?

✶

What might be most important
to you by then?

Question 9

Do you think you'll still have the same definition of success when you're in your fifties and sixties?

I know it might feel impossible to imagine your life in several decades' time! The reason for trying to do it is that thinking about how you might want to be in the future can help you clarify your goals for now. What you want your life to turn out like overall can help you to decide what you need to start doing – you have to know what you want before you can actively work towards it! By figuring out what you think a successful life would look like in thirty or forty years, you can begin to prioritise how you spend your time and energy in the next few decades.

Of course, none of it is written in stone. Your ideas of a successful life are likely to alter as you grow and change. Often, it's only by following one path that we realise that it's not the path for us. But you can't find that out unless you start going in the direction that feels right at this point in time. If it proves not to be right for you, at least you know. Then you can follow your evolving ideas of what happiness and, ultimately, success mean to you.

What about the traditional status symbols of success, such as cars, particular clothes, jewellery, big houses, high-profile careers, or exotic holidays? Of course, you can strive for them and enjoy and appreciate what you have of them. But they are badges of financial success only, which is a very narrow definition to base your life on. Any happiness they bring is usually temporary, and while they can be fun and satisfying at the time and can bring great experiences, what proportion of your time and energy do you want to put into pursuing them, just for the sake of having them? As you get older, the value you see in them is likely to diminish for you.

After living several decades of life, I feel that I could have done a lot better, and I could have done a lot worse – in terms of achieving these status symbols. I feel, though, that as long as I have a roof over my head, enough to eat, my health, and people I love in my life, the rest aren't things that give me a feeling of success or accomplishment in life. I enjoy them, but I feel like my life gets more successful every day through connecting with the people around me and continuing to strive to live completely as myself. That feels good.

Would it be about who you were
as a person? Your career?

✶

Do you think it would matter more
to you how many people were there,
or that the ones that were there
knew you well?

Question 10

What would you like people to be saying about you at your funeral?

And you thought Question 9 was a hard one to answer! I know this is a difficult one to hit you with at your age. It might be the first time you've been asked this, but it's an exercise that comes up often in self-development books and on courses. The great thing about answering it is that it helps you get clearer on what's most important to your future, out of all your hopes and dreams, and from all the ideas that you've come up with about what might feel like success. It's about getting to realise what you value above all in life.

That's what becomes apparent when you have to narrow it all down to the few things that, most of all, you'd want your life to have been about by the time you die – hopefully at a ripe old age. Just beginning to consider these things now will make you more aware of them as you go through the various stages of your life. They can become the core goals that you keep returning to, checking how on track you are with achieving them, at times when you feel a bit lost or directionless.

The relative importance of various aspects of your life is likely to shift over time, but for most of us, the central theme is likely to be around relationships. People need people. Whether it's family, carers, friends, colleagues, or a partner, our relationships are usually where we leave the biggest imprint in our lives.

I don't know what my answer to this would have been at your age. Over the years though, I've thought about it several times. The two things I feel I'd regret most would be if I got to the end of my life and I hadn't been able to live as my authentic self and hadn't lived my life to the full. At my funeral, all I would want is for the people I love to be remembering all the times we've shared – when I'd made them laugh or held them as they cried. I'd want them to feel that they knew the real me and, even more importantly, could be their real self around me, and that I knew the real them. I think that would be the result of a life well lived. A life of love.

Has it been rigid and structured
or relaxed guidance and support,
or somewhere in between?

✶

Are there a lot of rules, shoulds,
and shouldn'ts that you've had
to live by?

✶

Have you felt constrained
by any of these?

Question 11

How much do you feel you've been moulded and conditioned by those around you growing up?

Some of our societal and family conditioning is obviously a good thing. It helps us to understand more about life, relationships, and how the world works. It can keep us safe, help us to communicate better, and save us time and energy having to figure out some things for ourselves so we can function more easily in the world. There is a 'but' though. Others often expect us to stay the same person, even though we all change and grow throughout our lives. And as we head towards becoming an adult and start figuring out who we are as an individual, that conditioning can feel too restrictive.

When that conditioning is telling us who we are, it can feel particularly disempowering. Whether it's from parents or carers, learning institutions, or even our friends, we're reminded of our particular traits and idiosyncrasies on a regular basis and are often pigeonholed by the way everyone sees us. Then we usually live up to this by being who we think we're supposed to be – who the people around us have told us we are. In her brilliant book *Untamed*, author, Glennon Doyle, talks of this as our taming. What if this doesn't match who you feel you truly are underneath? What if you've grown out of some of the labels or roles, but others still want to attach them to you? Do you risk the possible discomfort, to yourself and others, of showing that these aren't who you are anymore, and maybe they never were?

I didn't see all this until a lot further down the road in my life than where you are, but I always felt it. At your age, I felt constrained by the expectations on me to be a certain way – from my family, and even from wider society. It's taken me a while to work out what's the necessary stuff and what's the stuff that negatively impacts my life. Usually what causes problems for me is when I'm trying to be who other people expect me to be rather than myself, and when I'm not following my gut instincts on what's right for me to do or not do. It's definitely something we discover over time, but I hope you get a start on it a lot sooner than I did!

You can begin by trying to recognise the different ways in which you've been conditioned and notice the thoughts and feelings that arise in you when you reflect on these things. Then, over time, you'll discover which aspects of this conditioning feel okay for you, and which don't. You'll start to realise what rings true and serves you well now, and what belongs in the past.

If you do, is there a big difference?

✶

How would you describe the differences?

✶

Are you a different version of yourself
with different groups of people?

✶

With certain people, do you feel
that you can show more of the
inside you?

Question 12

Do you feel there's a you on the outside who the world sees and another you, inside, who is more hidden?

It's natural to have aspects of ourselves that we keep more private or just reveal to certain people. It can be scary to risk showing who our inside self is, and it's valid self-protection to only do that with people who we trust. It becomes less healthy though when we have big discrepancies between who we portray to the world and who we feel we really are inside, or when we feel we can't be our true selves with anybody. The bigger the difference, the more likely it is to affect us negatively – mentally, emotionally, and in our lives.

To start with, even just acknowledging that we have two different selves and exploring who the more hidden self is and why we feel we need to keep it hidden can lessen the negative impact. Often, just being honest with yourself can be a relief, even if you don't feel ready to outwardly express your inner self yet. Paying attention to who you are on the inside and noticing who you present yourself to be in the world, you begin to discover which feels truer for you. Getting to really understand what moves and motivates you helps you become more comfortable with yourself. Then you're able to objectively decide which aspects of that self you'd like to express more. Doing this, you are likely to feel more seen, and understood for who you really are. Ultimately, over time, who you are on the inside can become who you are on the outside too. Then you're living as an integrated, whole person. You are just one self.

When you do that, maybe some people won't like the truer version of you. Maybe others will love you more. That will also be the case if you continue to keep more of your inner self hidden – some will like you, some won't. Wouldn't you rather be liked – or not liked – for the real you, rather than who you think you 'should' be? You may have to deal with criticism – often others don't like it if we start to change. Maybe it makes them uncomfortable, or upsets the status quo. But the strength and sense of freedom that come from being your authentic self can help you deal with that. Those you love may come round when they realise that it's important to you to be who you really are.

This process has to be at your own pace. Its purpose is to help you feel more comfortable being yourself – stronger and more capable. It's not supposed to be something which causes you to feel too vulnerable or anxious. Work through it at the speed that feels right for you and be kind and compassionate to yourself as you do.

Is it a constant thread that runs through
your life but is more visible at
some times than at others?

*

Are you most fully yourself only
in particular situations,
or with particular people?

*

Is it something you feel you have
any control over?

Question 13

When do you feel that you are most fully yourself?

Before I came to know myself better, I couldn't have told you who my true self was. However, I did recognise that I experienced times – or moments – where I felt more relaxed, freer, less critical of how I was being in the world. At these times, I did have a sense that I was being more fully myself and that I was expressing this to whoever I was with or through whatever I was doing. It was usually just with two particular friends though who I felt knew the inner me as well as the outer me. But I don't think I ever recognised during those times that I was being my authentic self.

The more you get to understand yourself, the more you begin to trust in your authentic self and feel comfortable expressing that self in the world. Each step you take in this direction builds momentum over time and grows your own authenticity until it inhabits all of you. Our unique human ability to reflect on our thoughts, feelings, actions, and interactions enables us to do this. You're investigating the way you are and the way you live your life in order to change and grow.

Most children, when they are young, ask lots of questions. They ask them incessantly, for years! This stops as they get older. I think partly because they become more self-conscious – they don't want to appear stupid by not knowing things or are worried they'll become embarrassed. And also, I think, because societal norms and pressures sometimes curb curiosity. Now, as you enter adulthood, it's important to start asking lots of questions again, even if it's just to yourself. It's how you come to make sense of yourself and your world. You're learning in a whole new way now, as an independent adult, figuring out things in order to create the life you want to live. Self-questioning and paying attention to what answers come up for you helps you on that journey.

The more fully you feel you are being yourself, the less you have to worry about 'being' a certain way. You're not trying to fit into a mould of who you think you should be; you don't have to overthink it or have the tension between your inner and outer selves anymore. This creates a far more enjoyable experience of life for you that can bring with it feelings of freedom and empowerment.

Do you judge or criticise yourself
for what you do notice?

Do you imagine what others might
be thinking of you?

Question 14

How aware do you think you are of how you behave in the world and interact with others?

Often, especially around your age, we think we're self-aware when what we're actually experiencing is self-consciousness. Self-consciousness and self-awareness are two different things. When you're self-conscious, it's about how you feel you are seen by others, how you feel you might be being judged by them; you might feel nervous of being embarrassed. In doing this, you are outwardly focused on how you think you are being perceived. Or inwardly, you are judging and criticising yourself for either how you are or how you think you're seen to be. All of this is self-consciousness, not awareness.

Self-consciousness serves no purpose. It's a negative, destructive habit that we develop growing up. Often our self-judgements and criticisms come from our inner critic, which echoes the voices around us, or messages that we've absorbed from our life experiences. We then use those messages against ourselves, continuing to reinforce them. The sooner you can recognise this inner critic in your own head and shift away from it towards self-awareness instead, the healthier and happier you are likely to become.

Self-awareness is when you just notice how you are in the world, without self-critical judgement. You learn about yourself, and you might decide you want to do things differently but without beating yourself up about having done things 'wrong'. Awareness is reflecting on the things you say, the way you say them, how you behave, or how you look – but in a relaxed, curious way, as if you're trying to pull the pieces together for the jigsaw puzzle of you. You're just gathering information. Not judging yourself, not criticising yourself, not feeling bad about yourself because of what you see – only noticing what is going on for you just now. It's a learning process: you can't change and grow until you begin to see the reality of who and where you are now. That's the place where you begin becoming your truest self and can start going where you want to go in your life.

Nobody is ever all good or all bad, including you. As human beings we all have the capacity to be uncaring, destructive, judgemental, critical ... every 'undesirable' trait you can think of. We also all have the capacity to be kind, compassionate, generous ... every 'desirable' trait you can think of. Often the traits we display are a result of our life experiences and conditioning. As we get older though, we realise that we can actively foster the aspects of ourselves that feel most true for us.

Are you often conscious of your
mental and/or emotional state
in the moment?

*

Is it in the background or the
foreground of your awareness?

*

Does it cause tension within you
or are you relaxed with it?

Question 15

How much are you usually aware of what's going on within you – in your thoughts and emotions?

This type of self-awareness is trickier, especially when it comes to our emotions. Noticing how we're feeling often takes us into our heads. Then we start thinking about how we're feeling, instead of just feeling it: we judge it, worry about it, or want to distract ourselves from it. The trick, which you have to do consciously and have to repeat until it becomes habitual, is to let the feeling just be. To accept that, for whatever reason, this is what is going on within you at this time. When you do this, the feeling often subsides. It runs its course if you just notice it without latching onto it.

Sometimes, when strong emotions subside, you might want to reflect on what the feelings could have been about – again, in a gentle, relaxed way, not intensely in your head. You're aiming for awareness and acceptance of your emotional state. Noticing what bubbles up to get your attention so you know what's going on within you, not necessarily to do anything about it.

With thoughts, I've found a different approach tends to work better. Again, become aware of them by noticing them, not judging, criticising, or condemning yourself for having them. Then try to get a different perspective on what they are. These thoughts are rarely meaningful. They're nearly always repetitive, playing on a loop, and usually negative or, at least, not helpful. They are often around judging and criticising ourselves or others, or comparing ourselves or our lives to others. They come and go, almost continuously, in a tumbling sequence that we're barely aware of. Rather than trying to become aware of each individual thought, you're aiming to just notice your thought patterns. Notice how much you think about certain things, whether your thoughts are more negative or positive, if you're obsessing about something, or if your thoughts are often about the past or the future. I think of my thoughts as a radio station – I can tune into it if I want to, but otherwise, it's just background noise.

You can start creating a pause in these thoughts. Noticing your breathing is a good way to do this. Just concentrate on focussing on each breath in and out, not letting your mind pull you away from it. Another way is looking about you as an observer, taking in all the details of what's around in a relaxed way. In doing this, you interrupt being locked in your thoughts. The more often you can practise this, the easier it'll be to switch off from your thoughts when you need to. These are basic mindfulness techniques.

Do you tend to think a lot and often live in a tense state, or are you relatively relaxed, even when you're thinking about something challenging?

✶

When you need to make a big decision, are you more likely to think about it intensely or follow your gut instincts?

Question 16

Would you say that you live more from your head or your heart?

I believe that the more we live in our hearts, rather than our heads, the better it is for our health and wellbeing – mentally, emotionally, physically, and spiritually. How do you do that? You start to become aware of where you mostly live now.

Living in our heads gets us tense. We get locked into our thoughts – thinking, thinking, thinking everything to death. We ruminate on the past or worry about the future, rather than staying in the present. If we have to make a decision, we often go round in circles in our heads, analysing and problematising, for hours, days, or even weeks.

Living in our hearts, we function more on how we feel, what our emotions are telling us. We're aware of our emotional states. When making decisions, we're more inclined to go with how we feel, rather than what we think. I don't mean impulsively, in every moment – it's about being aware of which choices are aligned with what's most important to us overall, and which aren't.

Of course, most of the time, we go between the two. Our heads are caught up in the stories we tell ourselves about who we are, the labels we give ourselves or have been given, as well as the societal and cultural influences bombarding us daily. On the other hand, our heart is about love, compassion, empathy, passion, connection, community, instinct, and longing. It's what makes us human. We're not boxed, labelled, judged, or criticised by our hearts, and we don't do these things to others when living from our hearts. We do all of that from our heads.

Living from your heart doesn't mean always showing what's in your heart, not unless you want to. It's about knowing what's in your heart and paying attention to it while you go about your daily life. Over time, living more from your heart takes you towards knowing yourself better and recognising instinctively how you want to live your life.

Obviously, we still need to think! Our wonderful human brain can help us to implement all that's in our hearts. What is problematic for us is when we are locked in our head without connection to our heart. When our head rules us, we lose our connection to our truest self – we literally lose our self. Staying aware of what's in our hearts, we live as the authentic human being who lies at the core of us. This is the opposite of – and the antidote to – the materialism, consumerism, and superficiality that we see all around us.

What does creativity look like to you?

Is it just about being artistic
in some way?

Do you think everyone has creativity
in them?

Where do you think it comes from?

Is it something you can develop?

Question 17

Do you feel that you are at all creative?

In a nutshell, I see creativity as what we put out into the world, instead of what we pull in from it. It's a power within you, an energy that you can harness and direct towards what you do in life. Yes, it might be creating a piece of art, writing a book, making amazing cakes or playing a musical instrument, but it's also so much more. It might be in how you organise your living space, the ideas you have to improve things, the way you dress, or how you take action in the world. Anything that you do where you express your inner self in something other than conversation is creative. You are literally creating your world from your true self.

When you see creativity in this way, creating your own life becomes an adventure. Creativity isn't about doing things a certain way – there's no right or wrong. It's about exploration, trial and error, imagination, inspiration, passion, ideas, and what-ifs. When you learn to live more from your heart, your creative instinct doesn't talk to you in words, it reveals itself in urges and promptings, in knowing the right thing to do next, even if your head disagrees sometimes. Creativity is visible in your dreams of how your life could be.

The more you follow your creative urges, the stronger your creativity will become and the more you'll feel like you are putting yourself into what you do. As it develops over time, you'll start trusting in it to guide your direction. You'll also begin to see more of a connection between your true self and what you create in your life.

The absolute best thing about experiencing your own creativity is that when you're doing something that you're putting your true self into, you can get into a flow with it. Not always, but when it happens it feels great. You feel that you're doing what you're naturally meant to do as a human being – it just feels right. That feeling becomes a reward in itself, regardless of whatever you produce from your creative impulses. I've spoken to many other people who get the same feeling from creative expression.

We all have creativity in us. It's how we grow and change. It's about building instead of destroying, trusting our sense of knowing instead of analysing. It's about directing our inner selves to create the life we want by expressing who we are in the world. It's the lifeforce within us.

What does the word 'soul'
mean for you?

✶

Where might it reside in us?

✶

Where might it come from?

✶

Do you think we can develop
our connection to it?

Question 18

Do you believe that we all have a soul?

I believe we all have a soul. I can't prove it, or adequately describe or explain it, but I feel that it exists from my experience of connecting to my own soul. I recognise it in inspiration and ideas, in having a clear vision for the way forward, even when it often doesn't make sense in my head. It's in a feeling of connection to all of life and is always there for me to come back to when I need to feel more centred and grounded, a feeling that I'm something more than this flesh and bones.

It isn't a spooky or supernatural thing. It's isn't religious. It's something that most of us grapple with the idea of at some point. You'll come to your own conclusions, over time, in your own way. This is just where I've come to with understanding it, after years of soul-searching, study, and life experiences.

Here's the best analogy I've ever heard to describe what our soul is. Imagine humans are lamps. When we're born, we're plugged into our source of electricity – God, universal energy, spirit, lifeforce – whatever each of us prefers to call it. The more we use this energy, the more it will flow into us and illuminate our lives. We throw the light this energy generates out into the world, in all that we do. When we die, the lamp (us) is unplugged from the power source. The lifeforce that infused us is gone, and our body is the shell that's left. Whether that energy is still our individual spirit and somehow lives on eternally or just dissolves back into the universal lifeforce, I don't know – nobody does. I don't feel I need to know; I just focus on enjoying my connection to what I do understand.

I believe that our soul is where the creative lifeforce meets us as an individual and where we connect with it through our heart. When you live more from your heart, you begin to recognise and experience your soul. As you draw on it, it flows through who you are in your head, in your character and personality, and through the filter of your life experiences to date. These all affect how we then express that lifeforce in the world, how we create in the world. Creativity is your unique expression of your own soul.

The more you tune into the things that energise and inspire you, the stronger your connection to your soul will become. You'll live from it, trust in it, and create the life you're meant to. It's a process of trial and error. You move towards what feels right until it doesn't, then you adjust to what feels more right, picking your way towards what is right for you, next step by next step.

Do you focus more on your needs
or your wants?

✶

Do you have a vision for how your
life would be having these things?

✶

Do they have an order
of importance?

✶

Which of your needs are
already met?

Question 19

What do you think are the differences between your wants and your needs?

I hope that you were fortunate enough to grow up with a roof over your head, enough food to eat, and the care of people who loved you. If you did – and if others around you did too – then you're likely to have thought of these things as a given, not a privilege. Then, as you grew up, maybe you became aware of poverty and lack in the world – in other countries, or in your community. You might have felt sadness and compassion but were detached from it. On the other hand, if you've had direct experience of lack, you may have felt the divide between yourself and others who haven't experienced it.

The more we realise the basic privileges we have, that other human beings don't, the easier it becomes to separate our wants from our needs. When you see what you truly need as opposed to what you would like – your wants – you start to build appreciation and gratitude for all that you already have. It's not about feeling guilty if you've had the good fortune to be born into your family, in your part of the world, and have had all your basic needs met. Guilt doesn't serve any purpose. Appreciation and gratitude do. They have an abundance of positive power. When you carry them with you each day, you focus less on what you want and, in time, begin to look more towards what you can give than what you can get.

Of course, that doesn't mean you can't still strive for an even better life and enjoy nice things. It doesn't mean it's wrong to want more. But if you keep alive an awareness of all that you already do have as you strive for what you want, you'll enjoy the journey to get there a lot more, and your happiness won't depend on just fulfilling your wants.

It's also helpful to think about the levels of importance you give to your needs and wants. After the basics of shelter, food, and love, you might feel the need to focus on your physical, mental, and emotional health, to be able to live your best life. You might feel the need to develop yourself in some way, to help you become happier and more fulfilled. How much of your time, energy, and attention do you direct towards the things you need compared to your wants? Which are from your heart and which from your head? Ask yourself which will help you become your truest, best self and live the life you want to live. Then focus more of your time now, each day, on those – at the same time as keeping in your heart an awareness of all that you already have.

Big things, small things,
what are the things that
shape your life?

✷

What do you want to be different?

✷

Are there habits or behaviours
that you'd like to change?

Question 20

What would you like to do more of in your life, and what would you like to do less of?

This follows on from the last question about your needs and wants. If you're clearer on which are most important to you, then you can start to prioritise how you spend your time. Creating the life you want isn't about what you do in the future, it's about what you do now. In each choice you make, every day, you either move closer to what you need and want, or you press the pause button on the journey towards them.

Over the years, I've tried lots of ways of doing this. The best way I've found is to write down everything I know about how I ideally want to live my life. Then I'll write a list of what I need to do day-to-day to create all of this. This is my list of 'aligned actions'. I go back to it often and add or remove things. It's a shorthand for keeping me on track. At any time, I can give myself a 'stop and think' by asking, 'Is how I'm spending my time right now an aligned action?' If I'm feeling a bit lost or down, or lacking motivation, I can look at what I really want my life to be about and then do any aligned action on the list to start the process of getting back on track. Try it for yourself – it works!

Then you can think about the things you spend your time and energy on that don't take you towards what you most want. These are your 'non-aligned actions'! You've now got a clear distinction between the things that you need to do less of and those you need to do more of to take yourself in the direction you want to go.

Part of this is figuring out which things help you to stay connected to your authentic self and which make you lose yourself. For me, I've come to realise that I lose myself with the paralysis of overthinking when I go for the distraction of being locked in my head, or if I choose to overindulge in food, alcohol, or screens too often. We get into habits of doing things that make us lose ourselves because there are usually immediate rewards attached to these. However, these choices take me away from being myself. I press the pause button on the life I want to create.

On the other hand, in choosing to direct myself towards one of my aligned actions, I find myself again. Delayed gratification means focussing more on the long-term rewards rather than the immediate ones, and you can develop this ability.

Question 21

Who might your truest self be, and what would you like your life to look like?

No sub-questions here because this is a simple one, right?

Where do you start?

In case you hadn't noticed, you've been exploring the answer to this question in all the answers that you've come up with already. They've led you through looking at who you feel your real self is and how integrated that self is with who you present to the world. You've looked at what some of your fears are, how aware you are of your thoughts and feelings, and how you behave in the world. You've started to look at your wants and needs and to distinguish between the two. Then what you might want to do more of and less of.

These form the basis of realising who your truest self might be and how you'd like to live your life. Getting to know and understand yourself better is the start of coming to know what your true self wants. It's not just about your career or your relationships – it's more fundamental than that. It's about how you fulfil your unique potential as the human being you are which comes from knowing what you're passionate about, what's important to you, and the type of person you really are, in the core of your being, then staying aligned with that self. It's not about some fantasy of the perfect you or the perfect life that is often formulated by our conditioning and outside influences.

Get still and quiet, maybe by doing some basic meditating, and give yourself time to come out of your head and into your heart. When you feel relatively relaxed and calm, imagine yourself as your truest self. It might take time, and you might only get glimpses. On the other hand, you may have a strong, clear impression of who this truest self is already. Draw on your imagination, your heart, and your soul as you do this. Write it down. Reflect on it over a few days and keep coming back to it. It's not about changing yourself to become this person; you're drawing out the deepest version of the self that you already are. You are completely qualified to be that. And you don't need anyone's permission to be that person either.

As this authentic you, how would you be interacting in the world? What's the life you would be living? What work would you be doing? How would you dress? How would you spend your time? What would be important to you? It doesn't matter how far you think you are from it all, or how realistic or unrealistic you think it is. You're daring to dream of what you'd love to create. This usually changes over time. You're just making a start on knowing what you most want now. Then, when you have enough of a vision for your life to start with, work out what the initial steps would be for you to start going in the right direction. Write them down. A lot of it might come from the twenty answers you've already given.

Create a plan for yourself of what feels most important to start with. Remember, you don't have to do everything at once. Any steps you take in the right direction are progress, however small. Do something and build on it, then brick by brick, you lay the foundations on which you can build the life you want. This is living your life with purpose, as the most genuine version of you. It's not easy, but it's so worth it, and you are completely capable of doing it.

It doesn't matter if you change course at a later date; it doesn't matter if things don't work as you'd hoped. What matters most is that you're willing to keep getting to know who you are, follow the instincts of your truest self, and keep putting one foot in front of the other in whatever seems the best way for you now. Having a plan gives you no guarantee of creating it, but it does give you a direction and something to work towards.

Whenever you feel lost, confused, alone, or lacking in direction, keep returning to this process. Notice the promptings of your soul. If you keep doing that over and over, you'll be steering your life towards fulfilling your potential as a human being – and that's more than most people ever do. You owe it yourself to at least give it a try.

Epilogue

Thanks for working through this book. I really hope you got something from it that will be helpful to you in your life. I also hope you can see that, by working through the questions, you've followed a process of peeling back the layers of who you are to discover how you can live your life in the way that you most want to. I hope you were kind and compassionate to yourself as you worked through it and that you'll continue to be. We never harshly criticise and judge the people we love, the way we do ourselves, so treat yourself like *you* are someone you love. You can be a best friend to yourself: someone you can always rely on for comfort, support, compassion, and kindness.

If anything has come up for you while working through this book that is causing you any distress, please seek support. There are so many brilliant organisations out there that work with a whole array of issues. Explore which support might be best for you if you don't feel able to talk to someone you know.

In going through this process, you'll already know a lot more about being yourself and creating the life you want than most other adults – even people decades older than yourself. Most adults never understand that their experience of life can be transformed by just getting to know themselves a bit better.

A key thing in all this is to only ever compare yourself to who you were yesterday, not to others. This is the antidote to our social media dominated, superficially obsessed, critical, judgemental society. There are few certainties in life and the curveballs come thick and fast, but if you keep coming back to yourself, to the core of who you are, and the strength that comes from being true to yourself, you'll be reassured that whatever life throws at you, you'll have the strength in yourself to deal with it, as best you can, and learn from it in order to change and grow.

This has just been a starter. Continue questioning yourself throughout your life. Dig deep and get creative in coming up with the questions that you think you most need to ask yourself at any given time. What you come up with might surprise you! Be honest with yourself and just keep pulling yourself back on track no matter how often you find yourself adrift. Even after years of doing all this stuff, I have days where I manage it and days where I don't. In the main though, my experience of life feels a lot happier, healthier, and satisfying than it ever was before.

As you come to know yourself better, you'll also become aware of other people who are trying to do their best to be their authentic self too. There is a huge benefit to ourselves, as well as to our relationships, in attempting to see things from the perspective of others, and in respecting and supporting them on their journey, wherever they are with it. Often others are dealing with their own internal battles that we don't see on the outside.

I wish you lots of love, lots of luck, and joy on the journey towards fully experiencing life as the unique, wonderful human being who you already are. I want to leave you with an extract from a speech that I heard recently – a quote from an unknown author:

> *As you journey through life, choose your destination well, but do not hurry there. You will arrive soon enough ... And if, upon arrival, you find that your destination is not exactly as you had dreamed, do not be disappointed. Think of all that you would have missed but for the journey there and know that the true worth of your travels lies not in where you come to be at journey's end but in who you came to be along the way.*

To be continued ...

If you've got something from this process, there are loads of great books and online resources out there to help you continue on your journey towards greater self-understanding. When you browse them, notice what you're most drawn to, what might be best suited to you. Many of them are related to particular areas of your life so that you can focus on these more specifically, i.e. relationships, anxiety, self-esteem, or developing spiritual practices such as meditation or mindfulness.

For further related content and to connect:
Sign up for updates: **stuff@lynnbmann.com**
Facebook: **Lynn B. Mann and/or Being 21**
Instagram: **lynnb.mann and/or being.21**
Twitter: **@LynnBMann1**
Website: **lynnbmann.com**

Acknowledgements

Getting this book completed and published has been a team effort. Thank you to: Sam Boyce for her clever editing and support, Heather Macpherson at Raspberry Creative for the beautiful cover design, and Kat Harvey for her eagle-eyed proofreading. Thank you also to Mary Turner Thomson of WhiteWater Publishing who has been a fantastic mentor and friend throughout this process.

The input and feedback from Jack Mann and Iona Wilson during the initial shaping of the concept and content of this book was invaluable. Thank you both for that and for your further feedback. Thank you, also, to all who completed the online survey – you know who you are! Your feedback and responses were much appreciated and very helpful – for myself and hopefully for others too.

I also greatly appreciate the reader feedback from Louise Welsh and Donnie Maclean who cast a thorough eye over my work, giving me their generous and honest comments and constructive criticism. Thank you both.

Lastly, but of course not least, a big thank you to Annie, Jack, and Chris, for being so supportive of my writing life and putting up with me in general!

Survey Responses

The following are some responses from the online survey I conducted while writing this book. They are included here for reference, in case they are of interest to you.

Question 1 – Do you feel like you are an adult?

'I feel like I'm in no man's land between childhood and adulthood, like a teen playing at being an adult!'

'I feel more like an adult with my friends, and a child with my family.'

'I know myself better from all the experiences I've had: leaving the bubble of school, moving away from home, and meeting new people.'

'I feel like lots of positive changes have happened, but I can see that for some people it's a tricky time. They go a bit off the rails.'

'I think my perception of adulthood is based on a feeling of greater power, or ability.'

‘I only feel like an adult when I’m around children. I think I’m navigating a very confusing time, with no real direction or confidence in the decisions I make … hopefully that will come as I get older.’

‘I feel the ever-increasing weight of adult responsibilities, however in many more ways, I still feel like a child, or at least not fully an adult.’

‘I’d tell myself at sixteen to realise that you have to work hard for things; they don’t just happen.’

‘Appreciate how good you have it – you’re privileged to have all the opportunities that you have. Make the most of them.’

Question 2 – What would you say are the major concerns of your generation?

‘I worry because we’re all so preoccupied with our social image or fame or material things. I worry how we’re going to be able to get beyond that.’

‘How are we going to deal with environmental, equality, and poverty issues? They all seem so huge. Where do we start?’

‘I think insecurities about jobs and relationships, as well as the environment and global warming. There are more mental health problems in my generation, but that's partly because we understand about it better.'

'Our mental health. The threat of climate change and war as the older generation make bad decisions about them. Also, we're connected and social online but value image in these so much that we've lost real connection to the world and living and experiencing it.'

'Increasing automatisation, and loss of liberty because of big tech.'

'We have the prospect of being a generation made poorer by their parents' generation, due to decades of overconsumption, democratic decay, and an insecure job market.'

Question 3 – What would be the best thing that could happen to your generation just now?

'It would be great if people thought less about themselves and more about the big issues and other people. I think we're all quite selfish.'

'If there were more jobs, so that we didn't need to worry so much about finding one.'

'If social media could become a less prominent thing. Although there is an upside to it where you can connect with people more easily, there is a dark side to it too, from everyone feeling pressure to keep up with it, and its focus on image and status.'

‘A visible effort from the government to improve how we deal with rubbish, particularly plastics; and an active response to increasing education on anti-racism, and LGBTQ+ and gender issues.’

‘The end of nationalism in all its forms, and the threat of destructive trade wars that bring pain to society’s most vulnerable.’

‘If more was done to help the mental health of people my age.’

‘That we all agreed to stop social media. I don’t think we could though.’

Question 4 – What are your biggest fears for yourself about how the rest of your life might work out?

‘Not succeeding in my career, or my siblings dying before me.’

‘Being homeless at some time, not having a roof over my head.’

‘I’m most fearful of something happening to one of the people I love.’

‘I wish I knew that I was going to have a close relationship with someone, that lasted a long time. If I could be certain that I wouldn’t end up lonely, that would be good.’

‘It would be good to know for sure that you were going to stay healthy.’

'I'd want to be sure that I was going to be okay financially.'

'I fear that no matter how hard I try I won't be able to help the environment enough, or that the way we help to conserve wildlife turns out to be the wrong approach.'

'Not being happy. Doing something I can look back on and be proud of.'

'Dying young because of all the threats we're facing.'

'Middle-class mediocracy, detachment from society, poor health.'

'Finding someone I love. I'm concerned about coasting and leading a very average life.'

'I worry for the health of my family and that I won't reach my expectations for myself or find fulfilling work. I worry about the expectations around women to want to have a child.'

Question 5 – What are you most scared of in life just now?

'Failing Uni.'

'Not being financially successful enough in my twenties to give myself more options and freedom as I get older.'

'I'm scared I'm ruining the best years of my life being sad and stressed.'

'I worry I'll lose someone I love. I don't think my family can cope with more loss.'

'I'm scared I'm wasting this bit of my life.'

'The turbulent job market is my most immediate fear. Risks around my graduate role exist but are largely unknowns. Since I can't predict these unknowns, I can't prevent or mitigate them. There's not a whole lot of purpose to worrying though.'

'I'm scared I'll go through my twenties not knowing what I want to do.'

'That I'll waste opportunities I get by not making the right decisions.'

'I want to make the most of what I've studied, but I'm scared I won't know what I want to do with my qualifications when I get them.'

Question 6 – Do you think that difficulties in life can teach you valuable lessons?

'I would get things out of the way, especially if there is a bad outcome from not doing them. I wish I'd learned lessons in self-motivation earlier than I have though.'

'I'll get things out the way if I have a clear goal, or it's something I'm interested in.'

'Yes, you can learn lessons big time. If you run away from problems or difficulties, it's a road to nowhere.'

'When I look back, I can see that I've learned lessons from various things, but I didn't notice that at the time.'

'I don't seek them out, but I'm glad of them when I can see them.'

'Yes, even if they make me sad or change me negatively, I treasure the lessons and hold onto them for when I need them.'

'I'm quite good at avoiding difficult things, but I feel lazy and unambitious because of it, and I regret it. The real sense of achievement after completing something tricky is the most life-affirming feeling.'

'I think it can sometimes take years for the realisations to come.'

'One hundred per cent, facing adversity is the best way to learn. By tackling difficulties, you learn much more about life, yourself, and you can push your limits.'

Question 7 – What do you think having freedom is?

'I think freedom is feeling able to just be yourself.'

'Mental freedom is feeling happy and content.'

'It's not having to do what you're expected to do, but what you think is right for you to do. Deciding for yourself.'

'Judgement from others can curtail your freedom, so if you have a supportive family or friends, you have more freedom and confidence to do what you want to do and be who you want to be.'

'Freedom of expression and emotional freedom are very important ... allowing yourself the freedom to feel whatever you feel, even if it's sad, jealous, or angry.'

'I think freedom comes from releasing ourselves from the expectations of others.'

'Freedom is the minimum amount of constraints on how one lives life. Absolute freedom, where everyone can do as they please, would be no freedom at all. Some constraints are necessary for overall freedom and to avoid anarchy.'

Question 8 – What does a successful life look like to you?

'Being happy. Feeling like you've had a good life.'

'I think it's quite likely that having success in one area of your life might mean a lack of success in another. I'm not massively interested in financial success (privileged opinion). As long as I have a job that I consider an important way to spend my time, that I'm proud to tell people about, then I'll feel successful.'

'Being happy now, with what you have, even while you still pursue other successes or goals for your life.'

'Success = Happiness.'

'Being content and happy with life in terms of career, family, and friends.'

'Being in a good relationship, living as sustainably and comfortably as possible, and having made a significant impact on the progress against climate change.'

'Good relationships that make me happy would feel like success in life.'

Question 9 – Do you think you'll still have the same definition of success when you're in your fifties and sixties?

'Yes, the things that feel like success to me now – having people you love around you and being healthy – will feel even more important to a successful life then.'

'As long as I've made the most of the opportunities I've had and have no major regrets about not doing that, then I think I'll be able to look back on a life that feels successful.'

'I think when I'm older I'll be able to look back and realise that smaller moments were what made my life successful. That it was about softer emotional skills, rather than material and physical success.'

'I'll be more sure of my life path and hopefully more sure of myself.'

'It will depend on my financial situation, whether I'll be able to retire easily or not.'

'I hope so. I hope my current disdain for the excesses of wealth won't spite me when I'm living in a hostel.'

'I doubt I will. Financial commitments and the general demands of the modern world will likely warp my ideal. I hope the core persists though.'

Question 10 – What would you like people to be saying about you at your funeral?

'That I made other people happy. That I was fun to be around.'

'I'd most like to be thought of as a good friend.'

'I'd want them to say that I was a kind person, straight-talking and honest, but also empathetic and sensitive. I'd want them to acknowledge if I had a successful career. Most of all though, I'd want them to acknowledge I was valued and needed.'

'About the person I was, but whatever would help them mourn me.'

'Just a solid "he was an alright chap" would do. As long as my family and friends were there and proud of who I'd been.'

'The person I was, how I helped others, that I cared about other people.'

'Ambitious. Interested and interesting. Positivity that made those around him smile. Those are the qualities I most desire.'

'That I was full of life and always liked to surround myself with the people I love. That I was determined and honest and cared deeply for my friends and family.'

Question 11 – How much do you feel you've been moulded and conditioned by those around you growing up?

'It's a parent's job to shape you. If you had no guidance it would be hard to function in the world.'

'Everything shapes you. Your experiences and your friends shape you, as well as your parents and school. I think it's a good thing.'

'I've always felt constricted by having to "do the right thing". Until I left school and in the past couple of years, it's shifted to me being able to make my own decisions.'

'Sometimes I feel like I'm going against the rules that I've been brought up with, and it makes me feel guilty, but it doesn't stop me. If I'm not hurting anyone else, and it's what I really want to do, I just do it.'

'Some of the rules I've been taught are good to have, like being polite and kind, or treating others like you'd like to be treated. I wouldn't want to give them up.'

'I rebel against my parent's political views quite a lot. I think my parents tried their hardest with life lessons, but as a family, we're quite closed off emotionally.'

'I think my parents gave me freedom to think for myself – I didn't have many rules. My school shaping is being undone now for the better.'

'It's hard not to be, but with access to so much information online, in documentaries, social media etc., it's easy now to change your world-view to a less biased perspective.'

'On a basic level, I've adopted mannerisms from my parents, it takes real attention to even recognise them. I think it's everyone's duty to expand their experiences.'

Question 12 – Do you feel there's a you on the outside, who the world sees, and another you, inside, who is more hidden?

'Although I feel like I'm different with different groups of people, I feel like most of the time I'm showing my true self.'

'I know it's like that for a lot of people our age, that they hide a lot of themselves.'

'Definitely true. I present myself in different ways to different groups of people. I don't even know if there is a solid core of personality.'

'There is the side that the world sees, then a side that only I know, and my dearest friends who have seen me at my worst and know me better than I know myself.'

'There is a distinction. To get through life you have to put on a face. I hope the two are not too different. With those close to you there is no need for a face.'

'There used to be, now I'm more me with my family and friends. I'm learning who the real me is without societal conditioning.'

'Possibly. Social media in particular is very superficial. So people just think about and show their outside self, but that's not really them a lot of the time.'

'No, I'd say I'm pretty much as unfiltered as you can get. I used to be a more toned-down version of my inner self, but now, I'm all about expressing myself truly.'

'I'm harsher on myself than the world is. I see myself as stubborn, straight-thinking, and rather uptight. I fear not being valued or wanted, when in truth, I think people do actually quite like me.'

Question 13 – When do you feel that you are most fully yourself?

'It takes me a while of knowing someone, or a group of people, to feel comfortable enough to be myself. If I don't know people well, I don't think they're getting a true impression of me.'

'I would only feel confident enough to make a joke and feel fully myself with my closest friends.'

'You feel like you're being yourself when you feel able to say whatever you want. If you don't feel people are judging you.'

'Definitely more myself around my friends than my family. Not that I put up barriers around my family, but I feel my friends amplify my own personality.'

'When I feel secure with the people I'm with, or when I'm alone.'

'I often feel completely myself when I'm on my own or on a run, but when I do feel completely myself around my friends, I feel at my most content.'

'I'm myself in lots of different situations. When I'm alone I don't know if I'm a massive fan of the person I am.'

'I'm most myself when I'm having a laugh with my family. I'm often myself with my friends, but I think about what I say and sometimes change what I say.'

Question 14 – How aware do you think you are of how you behave in the world and interact with others?

'I'm not at the time, but quite often think about it afterward.'

'I'm not very self-aware. I think I would be more self-conscious if I was.'

'I think I'm too aware of it. It inhibits me.'

'I think it's useful to be aware of what we do, but if we constantly guard our words and actions, we can prevent the truth from coming out.'

'I think I'm usually aware, although sometimes I can speak before I think.'

'Yes, I think I have a strong sense of self-awareness, possibly verging on anxiety, in terms of how I portray myself to others.'

‘Yeah, I’m very conscious of how I’m coming across, to the extent that I can be dishonest about my beliefs to others.’

‘I’m constantly aware of how others will perceive me, and I act on that.’

‘I hope I’m aware of how I act, although I probably don’t recognise my own actions totally or interpret them as others do.’

Question 15 – How much are you usually aware of what’s going on within you – in your thoughts and emotions?

‘I’m pretty self-aware in the moment. But it depends what’s going on.’

‘I’m getting better at reflecting more on my own thoughts and feelings.’

‘It’s a way to get to know yourself better. I want that. Even if I don’t like what I find out, because I’ll know how I want to change then.’

‘I often feel confused or unsure about what I feel. I can be angry, upset, and happy, all at the same time, and can take it out on people around me.’

‘I find most of my feelings drift beneath the surface, and that it’s only when I’m experiencing potent emotions that I have any awareness.’

'Sometimes I pause and reflect on it. I sometimes write to get it all out.'

'I'm very aware and very self-critical, making it hard to have confidence.'

'No, I usually take a long time to realise my thoughts or emotions. I think I'm pretty perceptive at judging other people's emotions but not my own.'

'I think due to previous struggles I am extremely aware of when my emotional state changes and how to cope with these changes.'

'I notice what I think quite a lot, but I don't often know how I'm feeling.'

Question 16 – Would you say that you live more from your head or your heart?

'I'm quite impulsive. I think I much more tend to go with my instincts.'

'I think I do both depending on circumstances, but mostly, I probably live in my head.'

'My friends, who are an artist and a musician, definitely live more from their hearts. It's noticeable.'

'My heart prevails in most of my decisions, but my head works out the actions that will suit my heart's demands.'

'My head. I think about things and plan them out. I don't do spur of the moment at all.'

'Definitely my heart. I act on my emotions. Although sometimes I overthink things.'

'Head with some things, heart with others. I think my head makes better decisions.'

'Naturally I'd probably lead with my heart, but I think I've been sculpted by my parents to lead more with my head.'

'I think my heart needs a lot of direction and care. My decisions will ultimately be made by my heart but not without analysis in my head.'

Question 17 – Do you feel that you are at all creative?

'I think there's a strong correlation between living in your heart and being creative, that would make sense. You could maybe grow it if you learned to live more from your heart.'

'It comes from being passionate and excited about life. Having a drive and a zest for it. I think it definitely comes from your heart and that it's a power you could make stronger by being aware of it and using it to put into projects that you're doing.'

'There is probably a spiritual element to it, but I don't know how that would work.'

'I'm not that creative. I prefer logical things. I think we all have an element of creativity in us, but we choose to foster it, or ignore it, as we're growing up.'

'I like to think of myself as quite creative. I love listening to music and singing to myself, and I draw occasionally, and sometimes act and make short films. None of them are a standout talent, but I enjoy them. I think creativity is the best way to self-express and explore your own emotions.'

'Much more when I'm less stressed. It makes me happy and calm.'

'Somewhat creative, and I enjoy that, but it's more learned than natural.'

'I think I have creativity that I am yet to understand how to unleash.'

'I struggle sometimes with creativity, in comparison to my peers. I don't know if this is from how I was born or raised, but there's a tangible difference there.'

'I think it's based on personality. If a person is interested and independent, they're often creative. I'm too often drawn to immediate satisfaction and don't have the level of interest of a creative person.'

'I think we all have a will within us to do what we want and what we aspire to, but it's up to us to really pursue it and harness that.'

'I think following the things that make me happy will hopefully empower me.'

Question 18 – Do you believe that we all have a soul?

'I believe in it but can't define it, and I think that creativity could potentially come from your soul.'

'I don't believe in it. I think there is just electric signals in your brain that cause your emotions. I think creativity just comes from your life experiences. I don't think there is any spiritual element to creativity.'

'I think we do, it's part of what makes us human. I don't think it's completely separate from our bodies, it's what encompasses our morality and beliefs.'

'No, I don't. I'm massively perturbed by any hint of a supernatural or existential force that determines our lives. I think all people have a level of empathy, a sense of justice, and degrees of self-importance. The balance of those things determines character and might reflect what a spiritual person would declare a soul.'

'Not in the slightest. Unless the soul is something that makes us unique, then I would say it does exist, but I would prefer the term features to describe this phenomenon.'

'I think maybe yeah. I see it as more a shadow of ourselves.'

'The word 'soul' has such a convoluted meaning. I'm not sure. I think it is tied in somewhere with the so-called "moral compass".'

'I think a soul is a very ambiguous idea, but I do think we have one. I think few ever get to understand other people's souls in their entirety.'

'I think we must, but I don't understand it.'

Question 19 – What do you think are the differences between your wants and your needs?

'Your needs are the necessities of food, water, and shelter, everything else is wants.'

'I think obviously food and a home, but I think needs are also loving and being loved, and having at least a basic education.'

‘There are physical needs, but also mental and emotional ones.’

‘I think most of the time it feels like a blurred line between my wants and my needs. Sometimes I feel like I need something, but I don’t really.’

‘Thankfully, I have the luxury, as do most of us in affluent societies, of focussing my attention on my wants, as I have all of my needs.’

‘Our needs are what we must have in order to survive, but our wants help us to truly live – they are not all necessary and some are truly excessive or material.’

‘My needs tend to be more emotional things and my wants more physical.’

‘There’s a massive difference for me, being relatively privileged and middle class. Compared to the poorest ten per cent of the world, I’m sure I have everything and more of their wants and needs, but I take that for granted.’

‘Differentiating between needs and wants is quite snobby. Nobody needs anything; we all want a comfortable life with reasonable amounts of luxuries. The only differentiation should be between reasonable and over-indulgent wants, and those which can negatively impact those around you.’

'I think I focus on my wants to hopefully fulfil what I need to be happy.'

Question 20 – What would you like to do more of in your life, and what would you like to do less of?

'I'd like to do more adventurous things, to feel like I'm making the most of my life, not just doing work and basic life stuff.'

'I want to get less stressed by things. Just do what I need to do without the stressing.'

'I want to waste less time just sitting around passing the time, instead of doing something more enjoyable.'

'I would like to be able to laugh more and just enjoy simple things without worrying. I would like to spend less time thinking about the future.'

'I waste so much time on social media. I'd like to spend less time on it.'

'I'd like to do more meditation and work on myself more. I'd probably like to do less procrastinating too.'

'I'd like to do my academic work more. I would like to do less indulging (food, drinking, laziness).'

‘I’d like to overthink things less, and finally have a relationship.’

‘I’d like to work less and use my time recreationally more.’

‘I’d like to care less about how others think of me. I’d like to worry less about my body image. I’d like to do more things that I enjoy, instead of things I’m expected to enjoy at this age. I’m working towards these things every day in small ways.’

Printed in Great Britain
by Amazon

20985171R00075